American Community
Frontier Settlements

Raymond Bial

Children's Press®
A Division of Scholastic Inc.
New York Toronto London Auckland Sydney
Mexico City New Delhi Hong Kong
Danbury, Connecticut

Library of Congress Cataloging-in-Publication Data

Bial, Raymond.
  Frontier settlements / by Raymond Bial.
      p. cm. — (American community)
  Includes bibliographical references and index.
  ISBN 0-516-23705-5 (lib.bdg.)   0-516-25077-9 (pbk.)
  1. Frontier and pioneer life—United States—Juvenile literature. 2.
United States—Social life and customs—Juvenile literature. 3.
Pioneers—United States—History—Juvenile literature. I. Title.
  E179.5.B575 2004
  978'.02—dc22

                                                    2004005097

Cover design by Doug Andersen
Map by Robert Cronan
Photographs © 2004: Connor Prairie Living History Museum, Fishers, IN/Shawn
Spence: cover inset; North Wind Picture Archives: 4, 31; Raymond Bial: front
cover background, back cover, 1, 5, 6, 7, 8, 9, 10, 11, 12, 13, 15, 16, 17, 19,
20, 21, 22, 23, 24, 25, 26, 32, 33, 34, 35, 36, 37, 39, 40; Stock Montage, Inc.:
28; The Filson Club Historical Society, Louisville, KY: 30.

Contents

Journey into the Wilderness

From the mid 1700s to the late 1800s, thousands of homesteaders—men, women, and children—headed westward over the Appalachian Mountains. Leaving their homes in New England, New York, Pennsylvania, Virginia, and other eastern regions, they floated down the Ohio River by flatboat. They traveled along the Cumberland Trail by covered wagon through deep, shadowy woods. They usually started the long, slow journey in late winter so they could find a little land, build a cabin, and harvest a crop before cold weather came again.

They made their way into Kentucky, Ohio, Indiana, Illinois, and territories around the Great Lakes. Settlers came from many different places, but they shared a common wish to build homes for themselves on the frontier. Some looked for adventure, but most simply wanted to own a little land or a small shop and raise a family. Longing for a better life, they carved **homesteads** for themselves in the sprawling forests. Soon log cabins were dotting the forests. Most settlers farmed these homesteads. They raised livestock and grew corn and

Slow yet strong oxen pulled covered wagons to the homestead and were then harnessed to plows to break the soil for cornfields and gardens.

other crops. However, others came to provide goods or services to the homesteaders. Small villages sprang up, often along rivers and streams. Here, storekeepers, millers, **blacksmiths**, **coopers**, and schoolteachers came together on the frontier and formed new communities.

As soon as settlers had put in their first crops, they went to work building a one-room cabin to shelter the family in the coming winter.

Settlers often gathered to share large tasks, such as cabin raisings, corn huskings, and bringing in hay to feed livestock.

Homesteaders also came together to help one another with their work. In these gatherings, which were often called **bees**, they might clear land or raise a cabin for a newcomer. They might also help put up a barn. As time went by, there were husking bees and quilting bees. As the saying goes, "Many hands make light work." Survival depended on cooperation. As Englishman Charles Latrobe wrote after visiting frontier settlements in 1832, "A life in the woods teaches many lessons, and this among the rest, that you must both give assistance to your neighbor, and receive it in return, without either grudging or pouting."

Together settlers confronted the many dangers on the frontier, including blizzards, floods, and droughts; attacks from wild animals; warfare with native people threatened by the flood of settlers on their hunting grounds; and epidemics that swept through the frontier. Yet despite the hardships, they had come to make a new home for themselves, and they had come to stay.

Homesteads

Settlers could bring very few belongings with them. Conestoga wagons and flat-bottomed boats were just large enough for a family and a few belongings. Their lives depended on their bringing essential supplies and equipment and being able to make everything else they needed for survival. The frontier abounded with natural resources—wild game, wood, and fertile soil. But the pioneers still needed determination, hard work, and skill to provide themselves with food, shelter, and clothing.

After they arrived on the frontier, homesteaders usually waited several weeks, or even months, to put up a log cabin. First they had to hunt game, clear fields, and plant crops.

Survival depended on good tools, which included rifles for hunting game and spinning wheels for turning wool into yarn.

Pioneers spent many back-breaking hours chopping down trees to clear fields, build cabins, and provide firewood for keeping warm and cooking meals.

So, long after their journey was over, they continued to sleep in their wagons or tents. Or they built lean-to shelters known as **half-camps**.

One of the first things settlers did was to girdle trees—cut rings around their bark. This kept the sap from flowing up the trunks and killed the trees. As the leaves withered, sunlight reached the ground. With teams of yoked **oxen**, the settlers plowed and planted corn and other crops around the trunks. After the cornfield and vegetable garden were planted, it was time to build a cabin.

Although log cabins now seem as native to North America as the land itself, they were actually brought to the colonies by Swedish, Finnish, and German settlers. The earliest Swedish and Finnish cabins were made from round logs, sixteen to eighteen feet long, which were notched at the ends. German-style cabins had logs squared into timbers and carefully notched. These timbers fit more tightly than round logs, and the corners were neatly sawed off. The gaps between the logs were chinked—jammed with wood chips and sticks—and filled with mud or clay.

Sturdy German-style cabins were made of squared timbers with their ends notched so that the corners fit together tightly.

Swedish-style cabins were built with round logs—even cat-and-clay chimneys were often made of stacked logs.

An adze, saw, auger, and ax were all the tools a skillful and hard-working settler needed to build a log cabin.

This person is using a mallet and chisel to hollow out a log to make a wooden trough for watering livestock.

The ax was the settler's most important tool. Its blade kept very sharp, this handy tool was used to clear land, split firewood, and build cabins. Other useful tools were the broadax, adze, auger, hammer, saw, and froe. Homesteaders used a **broadax** to square logs and an **adze**—a tool with a long, slightly curved blade—to further smooth the timber. They used **augers** to drill holes for wooden pegs to hold beams and **rafters** together, as iron nails were very scarce. They drove pegs with a wooden hammer, or mallet. Settlers needed saws to cut openings for doors and windows. They used a froe, which had a slender blade set at a right angle with the wooden handle, to split logs into boards for shingles and door planks.

It was possible for a settler to build a cabin by himself with an ax as his only tool. However, if he had neighbors, he would usually have a "cabin raisin'." He might cut and trim the logs himself and lay the stone foundation to keep the logs off the ground and prevent rot. He would then invite his neighbors to stack the heavy logs and place rafters to form a pitched roof. With a little help, in a matter of days homesteaders could build a simple cabin, nestled in a valley or along a river.

Once the neighbors helped to place the heavy timbers, the family often finished the details—chinking the walls, setting the door, and shingling the roof. They covered the roof with overlapping boards or with **shingles**, called shakes, that shed the rain down their slopes. They covered the window openings—if there were windows—with animal skins or greased paper, which let only a faint light into the cabin.

Most cabins had dirt floors, which became hard-packed as people walked on them. Later, homesteaders laid a wooden

Pioneers split logs into thin boards called shakes, which were used to make a roof that shed the heaviest rain and snow.

With the help of a few neighbors to wrestle the logs into place, a settler could easily build a small cabin in just a few days.

floor of **puncheons**, or split logs, and covered the doorway with an old quilt or animal hide. When a sawmill opened nearby, they installed a plank door hinged with leather straps or iron hinges. A latch with a string through a hole in the door served as a lock. During the day, settlers pulled the string to lift the latch, but at night they withdrew the string to "lock" the door. Settlers told neighbors, "The latch string is always out," meaning visitors were always welcome in their home.

This cabin door has a simple wooden handle and a string that can be pulled from the outside to lift the latch on the inside and "unlock" the door.

The cabin also had to have a chimney—of stacked logs, stones, or handmade bricks. Because settlers were so busy, they often first made a **cat-and-clay** or **stick-and-mud chimney** of stacked logs. They shaped handfuls of clay and dried grass into rough bricks called "cats," which they dried in the sun. They stacked the bricks inside the chimney and plastered clay over them. The clay lining helped protect the logs, but these chimneys often caught fire anyway. So as soon as possible, settlers built fireplaces and chimneys of stones dug from their fields or gathered from a nearby streambed. If a brickyard opened nearby, they built a safe and sturdy brick chimney.

Homesteaders could bring little furniture with them. So the men made rough benches and tables by drilling holes in puncheons, and fitting them with wooden legs. They made bed frames with rough-hewn poles and springs of crisscrossed ropes. The ropes could be tightened with a wooden key, which led to the saying, "Sleep tight." Women made simple yet comfortable mattresses from dried cornhusks or grass, which they covered with quilts, blankets, and animal skins.

Although these cat-and-clay chimneys were lined with clay, the logs still got hot and sometimes caught fire.

Settlers had to make most of their furniture, such as this puncheon table and benches where the family gathered for meals by the fireplace.

Women carefully tended the fire, which warmed the cabin and heated iron pots of simmering soups and stews.

Sometimes people simply slept on buffalo skins and blankets spread on the floor, but as the saying goes, "A hard day's work makes for a soft bed."

As they didn't have closets, they stuck pegs in the log walls to hang clothing and other belongings. They often placed deer antlers over the door to hold their rifle—their most essential tool for survival. As Natty Bumpo, the hero in James Fenimore Cooper's novels, said, "If you're for a buck, or a little bear's meat, Judge, you'll have to take the long rifle, or you'll waste more powder than you'll fill stomachs."

The finished cabin was usually a single room, sixteen by eighteen feet—which served as kitchen, dining room, living room, workroom, and bedroom. It might have a loft, where as many as eight or nine children slept. Women kept a fire burning day and night. The fire provided both heat and light, although settlers also had homemade candles and sometimes oil lamps. If the fire went out they had to start a new one with a piece of flint or a pan of glowing coals donated by a neighbor. In the evening the family gathered around the fire for reading, sewing, and playing. The father told stories and the mother made corn-husk dolls while the children played with wooden tops or clay marbles.

Later, when settlers had more time, they chopped down trees on a few acres, cleaned up the brush, and invited neighbors for a "log rollin'." Nearby families came together for a day to pile the logs. The day's work was followed by a hearty meal and a big dance. They continued to clear land until they had carved a homestead out of the deep forest.

Settlers had to make almost everything they needed, including toys for the children, such as these cornhusk dolls.

Chores

On their journey west, settlers brought some tools, utensils, and furnishings for their homestead. Women might have essential cookware, such as iron pots, skillets, tin cups, and perhaps a few pieces of china. However, the settlers made or purchased most other household items. Boys and men carved wooden spoons and bowls. Butter churns, clay pots, iron horseshoes, and many other objects came from a craftsman at a nearby settlement.

Pioneer women had many tasks around the homestead. They not only cared for the younger children, but they also cooked, cleaned, and baked—and that was just the start of their chores. There was wool to be spun into yarn for clothing and carpets; there were candles to be made; clothing to be sewn and mended; eggs to be collected; butter to be churned; chickens to be caught, killed, and plucked; vegetables to be picked and cleaned; and meat to be salted (to keep it from spoiling) and stored for winter. They also helped out with the farm work, especially during harvesttime. Because women

Having brought few, if any, utensils with them, settlers carved their own wooden bowls and spoons used for preparing meals.

Among their many chores, women also made butter by repeatedly plunging this wooden tool up and down in a pot, or churn, filled with cream.

Girls had many duties, including spinning wool. Here, two children are cleaning wool that will be spun into yarn.

took care of the chickens and the milk cow, they traded eggs and butter in the village for household items.

Girls began to work at an early age. They fed chickens, washed dishes, and gathered greens during the summer. Girls learned to sew by age four and began to knit and to mend clothing. Older girls and women gathered eggs, carded and spun wool, salted meat, and made candles and soap. They tended vegetable gardens, milked the cow, made butter and cheese, sewed mattresses, and made quilts and warm woolen clothes.

Men also worked hard, especially in the early days, to carve a homestead out of the wilderness. They rose before dawn to tend to the livestock and prepare their tools for the day's work of clearing and plowing fields, sowing seeds, and cultivating their crops. The survival of the family depended on a good harvest.

Young boys fed livestock and gathered firewood. At a young age boys learned how to herd cattle, yoke oxen, handle horses, tend crops, and cut hay with a scythe. Older boys and men cut down trees and cleared land, lugged stones from fields, plowed, planted, built fences, harvested crops, sheared sheep,

Boys helped their fathers with chores around the farm including feeding the work-horses, grooming them, and harnessing them to wagons.

Girls helped their mothers in making soap, which was used for washing clothes and dishes as well as hands and faces.

and slaughtered livestock. They dug wells, raised barns and outbuildings, and made furniture and tools.

Families did much of this work themselves. At other times, they gathered not only to raise cabins and barns, but to saw firewood, husk corn, make cider, and butcher hogs. In the spring, they tapped trees for maple syrup and sheared sheep. In the winter, women enjoyed quilting bees. They also got together for candle making, soap making, and wool spinning. They shared news and stories, told jokes, and swapped recipes. After the work was done, the family enjoyed a large

When their work was done, people had a little fun singing and dancing to music played on fiddles, banjos, or guitars.

meal then played at sport contests and games. An old man might bring out a fiddle, and there would be singing and dancing. These events were a welcome break from hard lives in isolated cabins on the frontier.

Pioneer Games

When their work was done pioneer children enjoyed many kinds of games with wooden toys, string, and their imaginations. Sometimes an adult might craft toys, which might be sold at a village shop. However, most often, if children wanted a toy, they or their parents would have to make it themselves.

Children played a lot of games that kids still play today, though many of the games have changed. In drop the handkerchief, which was the same as duck, duck, goose, one child walked around a circle of children and dropped a handkerchief on a player, who then chased the first child. Similar to Marco Polo, blindman's bluff, was played in different ways: players either called out, as in Marco Polo, or remained silent. Either way, the blindfolded person had to find and tag another and then try to guess who the player was.

Often if a child wanted a toy, he simply made it for himself, like this boy, by whittling a piece of wood.

Children and adults played many games, such as a rousing game of checkers, that are still enjoyed by people today.

Pioneer children often got together with bat and ball in an open field for a game of rounders.

In hunt the shoe, a player sat in the middle of the circle as the other players passed shoes around behind their backs. The player in the middle then tried to guess whose shoe matched the shoe he was holding.

Children played leapfrog just as it is played today. They stood in a line, put their hands on their knees, and bent over. The last player then leaped over each person. When the leaper got to the front of the line, the last player then began to jump over the others. Children played rounders, which was similar to baseball, and shuttlecock, which is now called badminton. Occasionally they played stickball, a Native American game that has since become lacrosse.

Pioneer Food

In the early days, **pioneers** often struggled to get enough food. They hunted and trapped animals, caught fish in the rivers and lakes, and gathered herbs, roots, and berries from the meadows and forests. But most of their food came from their fields, gardens, and livestock. They grew corn, vegetables, and

People sometimes kept a flock of geese, which provided soft down feathers for bedding and meat for food.

Women baked johnnycakes in iron pots called Dutch ovens, which were covered with a lid and hot coals.

In summer, people ate fresh vegetables, such as green beans, which were snapped and cooked in stews and soups.

fruits. They raised pigs, cows, sheep, goats, chickens, ducks, and geese.

Most recipes used very basic ingredients, so the food often didn't have much flavor. Yet, as people often said, "Hunger makes the best sauce." For most of the year, they relied on salt pork, cornmeal, potatoes, milk, cheese, and butter. In the morning people often ate cornmeal mush or cornbread, known as johnnycake. During the spring and summer they added maple syrup, honey, fresh greens such as dandelion leaves, and vegetables from their gardens. During the fall, children

Women sliced apples and baked them into delicious pies, which were cooled in the breeze by the window.

enjoyed baked apples and apple pie. During the fall and winter they hunted deer, rabbits, partridge, wild geese, and ducks. Men tried to shoot a big turkey for special occasions like Christmas. They always considered themselves lucky to find a bear, which provided meat, fat, and a thick pelt.

Meat from deer, which was called venison, and livestock were often preserved and stored for the winter, as were dried apples and root vegetables, including carrots, onions, and potatoes. Settlers had to salt or smoke meat to keep it from

spoiling. They salted pork and smoked hams and sausages.
They didn't have refrigerators, so they cut blocks of ice from
ponds and lakes in winter and stored them in icehouses. They
used the ice in summer to chill meat and milk. Fresh milk
was also kept cool in the summer by putting it down a well or
into a nearby stream.

Daniel Boone and the Cumberland Gap

One of the best-known communities on the frontier was
Boonesborough, Kentucky, which was established by Daniel
Boone. Born in 1734, Boone grew up in Pennsylvania but
moved with his parents to the North Carolina frontier when he
was eighteen. In 1756, he married Rebecca Bryan and raised
ten children with her—when he wasn't away on the frontier.
He became the most admired of all frontiersmen. A friend
later said he was "a noble and generous soul, despising
everything mean."

Daniel Boone led the first group of settlers west of the Appalachian Mountains through the Cumberland Gap into Kentucky.

Of his many adventures, Boone is best known for blazing the Cumberland Gap. The Appalachian Mountains were a great barrier to westward migration. However, carved by wind and water, the Cumberland Gap at the borders of Tennessee, Kentucky, and Virginia formed a break in the mountains. First used by game animals and Native Americans, the Cumberland Gap became the best route for settling the territory between the mountains and the Mississippi River.

Almost ten years before Boone, Captain James Smith had explored the Cumberland Gap. Later he wrote in his journal, "We started just as the sun began to gild the tops of the high mountains. We ascended Cumberland Mountain, from the top of which the bright luminary of day appeared to our view in all his rising glory; the mists dispersed and the floating clouds hasted away at his appearing. This is the famous Cumberland Gap."

Boonesborough was established by Richard Henderson and Daniel Boone of the Transylvania Company. In 1775 Boone led the first group into the region where they put up several log cabins in a hollow of sycamore trees near the Kentucky

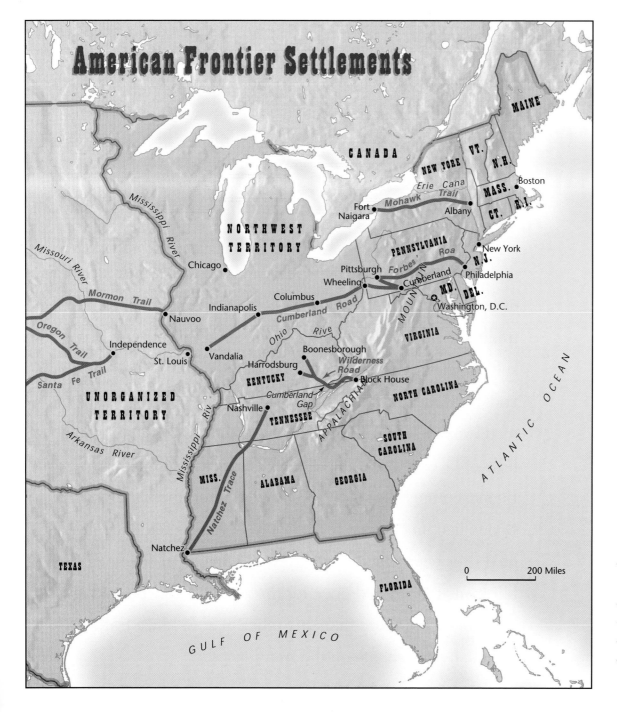

American Frontier Settlements

CANADA

MAINE

NEW YORK

VT.

N.H.

MASS.

CT.

R.I.

Boston

Erie Cana

Trail

Mohawk

Fort
Naigara

Albany

NORTHWEST
TERRITORY

PENNSYLVANIA

Roa

New York

Forbes

N.J.

Chicago

Pittsburgh

Philadelphia

Wheeling

Cumberland

MD.

DEL.

Columbus

Cumberland Road

Washington, D.C.

Indianapolis

MOUN

Mormon Trail

Ohio

Rive

VIRGINIA

Nauvoo

Oregon
Trail

Boonesborough

Independence

Vandalia

Wilderness
Road

St. Louis

Harrodsburg

Block House

Santa

Fe

Trail

KENTUCKY

NORTH CAROLINA

UNORGANIZED
TERRITORY

Cumberland
Gap

Nashville

APPALACHIAN

Arkansas River

TENNESSEE

SOUTH
CAROLINA

Mississippi
Riv

MISS.

ALABAMA

GEORGIA

ATLANTIC OCEAN

Natchez Trace

Natchez

TEXAS

FLORIDA

0   200 Miles

GULF   OF   MEXICO

Mississippi River

Missouri River

This map shows the
route taken by settlers
venturing westward into
the Kentucky frontier
where Boonesborough
was established.

River. Henderson later moved the settlement to a rise on the riverbank. In September 1778, the settlers built a **stockade** to protect their cabins—just before they were attacked by Indians and Frenchmen. The stockade helped the settlers fight off a nine-day siege.

Daniel Boone later moved on to Missouri. He said of himself, "Sometimes I feel like a leaf on a stream. It may whirl about and turn and twist, but it is always carried forward." However, over the next fifty-one years, Boonesborough stood as a trading center and a stopping point on the Kentucky River for settlers moving into the interior of the country. Between 1775 and 1810, two hundred thousand to three hundred thousand men, women, and children, crossed the Gap into the green hills of "Kentuckee" and later Indiana and Illinois. However, Boonesborough itself declined and ceased to exist by 1820. Boone had since gone to Missouri. When asked once if he'd ever been lost, he said, "No, I can't say I was ever lost, but I was bewildered once for three days." Bewildered or not, Boone did more than any other man to blaze trails and establish settlements on the frontier.

The log walls and blockhouses at Boonesborough protected settlers from attacks by Native Americans, whose hunting grounds they were invading.

Settlements

Over time, communities came to be established on the frontier. Sandford C. Cox, who settled in the Wabash River in the Indiana Territory in the early 1820s, later wrote that settlers, "cleared lands, rolled logs, and burned brush, blazed out paths from one cabin to another." As more arrived, a village was often established with a **gristmill,** where men took their grain to mills to be ground into flour or sold. People also needed a sawmill and various shops—a blacksmith, cooper, potter, and sometimes a weaver. They also needed a general store, a school, a church, and maybe a good doctor. As the village grew, a bank, a law office, and maybe even a post office would be established.

Many frontier settlements formed militias of men who came together to fight the bands of Indians that sometimes attacked the homesteaders. They also built a stockade as protection against these attacks. These forts had vertical log walls and one or more log buildings called **blockhouses** on the corners. It was nearly impossible to get inside the walls. Settlers cut

Here, men are using a pair of oxen to remove a large boulder. Clearing a field was backbreaking work.

The frontier could be a dangerous place. Many settlements were surrounded by forts like this one that protected families from attacks.

small openings, or "loopholes," in the blockhouse timbers, from which they shot their rifles at attackers. The second story overhung the fort walls so that they could actually shoot down on any attacker who tried to hide next to the wall.

If endangered, people abandoned their cabins and fled into this stockade. "I well remember," Joseph Dodridge wrote of his childhood, "how the family were sometimes waked up in the dead of night . . . with a report that the Indians were at hand. . . . The whole family was suddenly in motion. My father seized his gun and other implements of war. My stepmother waked up and dressed the children. . . . We caught up what articles of clothing and provision we could get hold of in the dark, for we [dared] not light a candle or even stir the fire. All this was done with the utmost dispatch and the silence of death."

When jammed into the stockade, the men organized a defense. There was the bang of rifles, the choking smoke of gunpowder, and the cries of children. People often went hungry and thirsty, but their very lives depended on fending off the attackers.

Once a sawmill was established on a nearby river or stream, pioneers were able to build homes with planks.

As soon as possible, pioneers built a sawmill, which provided lumber to construct other buildings in the village and nearby homesteads. Before the sawmill went up, logs had to be cut and shaped with axes and handsaws.

Within a few years, settlers were able to build plank houses held together with nails. With two stories and three or four rooms—all with wooden floors—these houses were often much larger than the cabins. The roofs were covered with cedar shingles and the wooden doors fitted with iron hinges. People even put in windows with glass panes called **lites**.

Grinding corn and other grains by hand with a mortar and pestle was hard work, requiring long hours of pounding.

The plank homes were heated with a stone fireplace or perhaps an iron cookstove with pipes to vent the smoke. These houses were furnished with cupboards, tables, chairs, and beds. However, water still had to be carried from a nearby stream, a well, a cistern, or a rain barrel.

Pioneers ate bread nearly every day. To make bread they had to grind corn, wheat, oats, or rye into flour. Early settlers ground kernels of corn and other grains by hand, usually with a mortar and pestle. However, this was a long and hard task.

As soon as possible, folks built a gristmill. Located along a stream, the gristmill had machinery that readily ground large amounts of grain. Water flowed over the paddles of a wooden wheel, making the wheel turn. The gears and rods connected to the waterwheel rotated and turned heavy grindstones, which ground the grain into flour.

A highly skilled miller was needed to run the gristmill. He had to know how to grind the grain properly and repair all the machinery.

Another essential craftsman in the frontier village was the blacksmith. He made useful objects mostly out of iron, which

When a gristmill was built, people brought their corn, wheat, barley, and oats there to be ground into flour.

is black, thus he came to be called a blacksmith. In this hot and tiring job, the blacksmith relied mainly on several key tools: a forge, a bellows, tongs, a hammer, and an anvil. Fired with coal, the forge was a very hot furnace used to heat and

The blacksmith crafted many useful iron tools, including horseshoes and hinges, that the homesteader could not make himself.

soften iron. The blacksmith pumped the bellows to blow air into the forge to make the fire very hot. With the tongs, he then held a piece of metal in the fire until it glowed bright orange. He hammered the hot iron into shape on an anvil, a block of iron with a flat top and pointed end.

The blacksmith crafted many very useful tools for the homesteaders, including nails, horseshoes, hinges, hooks, and cooking utensils. The blacksmith also tacked horseshoes onto the hooves of horses. However, a skilled worker known as a farrier often did this work. Women used iron hooks made by a blacksmith to hang iron cooking pots over the fire in the hearth. They could also stick a slab of meat onto the sharp points and roast it slowly over the fire.

The general store bustled as a trading center and meeting place for anyone who lived in the village and surrounding area. Pioneers had little or no money, so they usually traded, or bartered, their surplus crops or handcrafted objects for needed supplies. Folks also came to the store to share news, idle away a few hours, and play games such as checkers.

Settlers usually traded butter, milk, eggs, wool, maple syrup, honey, and hides for food items, such as flour, rice, brown sugar, coffee, spices, and molasses, which they couldn't provide for themselves. They traded deer hides, or buckskins, and so the term buck came to mean a dollar's worth of goods. They might also barter for some patent medicine, especially if there wasn't a doctor in the community. Settlers traded for china, buttons, silk, cloth, brooms, jugs, and iron goods made by the blacksmith. They also needed rifles, gunpowder, bullet molds, hunting knives, cooking pots, needles, awls, and other goods. Brooms, jugs, and iron goods might be made in the village, but everything else had to be shipped to the store by wagon or boat.

The shelves of the general store were filled with many wonderful goods, including bolts of cloth and housewares.

Settlers often traded their own products from farming and hunting —even deer skins—for goods available at the general store.

37

A village was fortunate if it had a doctor, whose house often had a special room where he treated patients. The doctor would also travel many miles out into the country on horseback or by buggy to help people who were too sick to come to the settlement.

Many diseases plagued the settlers, such as ague, or the "slows," which is now known to be malaria. Epidemics of typhoid, smallpox, and cholera broke out on the frontier. Most are now rare or easily cured. At the time, people believed that many diseases were simply caused by poisons in the blood. So they visited the doctor for a bloodletting. He made a small cut in the neck or wrist and let some blood drain into a bowl, which only further weakened the patient.

Many villages did not have a doctor, so the barber might do the bloodletting. If someone had a toothache, the blacksmith pulled it out with a pair of tongs. He did not use an anesthetic, or painkiller, to numb the jaw.

Settlers also treated their own aches and pains with home remedies. They washed sore eyes with cold chamomile tea. If they had a stomachache, they drank basil tea, and if they had

This is a one-room schoolhouse, with benches along one wall where students of all ages sat and recited their lessons.

a headache, they chewed willow-tree bark. They rubbed horseradish juice on aching feet and smeared sweet basil on wasp stings. These home remedies generally worked, so people had an herb garden and gathered wild plants.

At first, children went to school in a settler's home, the general store, or the village church. As the village grew and people had more time, they built a schoolhouse—usually a log cabin with a fireplace at the end or a potbelly stove in the middle. There was a dirt or puncheon floor, and the windows

Writing paper was expensive, so children often did their spelling and reading assignments on slate boards.

were covered with greased paper. The students sat on two or three rows of puncheon benches and worked at a big table.

Children learned "the three Rs" of reading, writing, and arithmetic. Their parents had not only to put up the building, but pay the teacher and buy school materials such as slates, paper, ink, and quill pens. These early schools had few books and other supplies. They were called "blab schools," because students learned by reciting their lessons out loud.

Children carried their lunch to school in a cloth bag or metal box. All the food came from their farm and garden: homemade bread, cold meat, muffins, hard-boiled eggs, cheese, jam, oatmeal or gingerbread cookies, pickles or preserves, garden vegetables (carrots, celery), and fruit (apples, pears, plums). They might also bring a clay jug of milk, apple juice, or cider. Sometimes the teacher made a big pot of stew or soup on the stove, which the children shared for lunch.

Schools were very strict. Children had to respect and obey the schoolmaster and accept punishment. They had to be silent during classes and speak only when called upon or when absolutely necessary. They were not to disturb other students, but get along well and help one another. They could not leave their seats without permission and then had to go quietly in and out of the school. If asked by the teacher, they had to bring in firewood, straighten the benches, sweep the room, and dust the school. They had to wash their hands and faces—and their feet if they came to school barefoot.

Before a church was built, settlers gathered to worship in small groups in a cabin, the general store, or the schoolhouse. When many people of the same faith moved to or near a village, they erected a church. However, there were few ministers on the frontier, so circuit preachers traveled from one village to another.

Over time the settlement might fade away as other communities prospered on the frontier. Some villages, however, grew into towns. Others became large cities, such as Louisville, Chicago, and St. Louis. The frontier moved westward across the Mississippi and onto the Great Plains. The children of the settlers were no longer pioneers, but the first generation of immigrants, struggling to make a new home in a new land.

Here's a rhyme that children recited to learn multiplication:

Twice times one is two.
This book is nearly new.
Twice times two is four.
Lay it on the floor.
Twice times three is six.
We're always playing tricks.
Twice times four is eight.
The books are always late.
Twice times five is ten.
Let's do it all again!

Glossary

adze—sharp-bladed tool shaped like a hoe for smoothing the surface of timbers

auger—hand tool for drilling holes in timbers

bee—gathering in which neighbors help one another, for example: a quilting bee (to make a quilt) or a house-raising bee

blacksmith—person who made things out of iron, such as spikes, nails, hinges, latches, horseshoes, and wagon wheels

blockhouse—log building on the corner of a stockade or fort

broadax—ax with a short handle and wide blade for squaring logs

cat-and-clay chimney—chimney of stacked logs lined with clay; also known as stick-and-mud chimney

cooper—person who made barrels

gristmill—mill that grinds grain into flour

half-camp—temporary lean-to shelter used by settlers

homestead—small farm established by settlers on the frontier

lites—glass panes in windows

oxen—cattle used for pulling wagons and plowing fields

pioneer—first person to settle in an area

puncheons—logs split in half and used to make floors and furniture

rafters—boards or beams that form the roof structure of a building

shingles—split wooden boards used to make a roof

stick-and-mud chimney—chimney of stacked logs lined with clay; Also known as a cat-and-clay chimney

stockade—small fort

Time Line

Daniel Boone leaves Kentucky for "elbow room" in the Spanish territories west of the Mississippi, settling near St. Charles in Missouri.

The first Transcontinental Railroad is completed when the Central Pacific and Union Pacific Railroads meet in Promontory, Utah.

The Treaty of Paris ends the American Revolution and extends U.S. border to the Mississippi River.

Lewis and Clark begin their expedition west, recording their discovery of different Native American tribes, rivers and mountains, and hundreds of plants and animals.

Frontier hero Daniel Boone (1734–1820) is born.

The Civil War begins.

1734 — 1775 — 1783 — 1787 — 1799 — 1803 — 1804 — 1812 — 1815 — 1861 — 1862 — 1869

Daniel Boone and Richard Henderson of the Transylvania Company journey through the Cumberland Gap and establish Boonesborough in Kentucky.

President Thomas Jefferson closes a deal with France on the Louisiana Purchase, which doubles the size of the United States.

The War of 1812 drives the British from most of the western frontier.

President Abraham Lincoln signs the Homestead Act, allowing settlers to acquire up to 160 acres by working and living on the land for five years.

The Northwest Territory is established, including the present-day states of Ohio, Indiana, Illinois, Michigan, Wisconsin, and part of Minnesota.

Find Out More

Children's Books

Bial, Raymond. *Frontier Home.* Boston: Houghton Mifflin, 1993.

Calvert, Patricia. *The American Frontier.* New York: Atheneum Books for Young Readers, 1997.

Duncan, Dayton. *People of the West.* Boston: Little, Brown and Company, 1996.

Josephson, Judith Pinkerton. *Growing Up in Pioneer America, 1800 to 1890.* Minneapolis: Lerner Publications, 2002.

Kalman, Bobbie. *Pioneer Life from A to Z.* New York: Crabtree Pub. Co., 1998.

Kallen, Stuart A. *Life on the American Frontier.* San Diego, CA: Lucent Books, 1999.

McKain, Mark. *Pioneers.* San Diego: Greenhaven Press, 2003.

Morley, Jacqueline, David Antram, and David Salariya. *You Wouldn't Want to Be an American Pioneer!: A Wilderness You'd Rather Not Tame.* New York: Franklin Watts, 2002.

Patent, Dorothy Hinshaw. *Homesteading: Settling America's Heartland.* New York: Walker, 1998.

Ritchie, David. *Frontier Life.* New York: Chelsea House Publishers, 1996.

Senzell, Sally. *Life on a Pioneer Homestead.* Chicago: Heinemann Library, 2001.

Taylor, Sherri Peel. *Pioneers of the American West.* San Diego: Lucent Books, 2002.

Wadsworth, Ginger and Shelly O.Haas *Laura Ingalls Wilder.* Minneapolis: Carolrhoda Books, 2000.

Warren, Andrea. *Pioneer Girl: Growing Up on the Prairie.* New York: Morrow Junior Books, 1998.

Whitman, Sylvia. *Children of the Frontier.* Minneapolis: Carolrhoda Book.

Places to Visit and Web Sites:

Conner Prairie
13400 Allisonville Road
Fishers, IN 46038-4499
Phone: 800-966-1836
www.connerprairie.org

Hale Farm & Village
2686 Oak Hill Road
P.O. Box 296
Bath, OH 44210-0296
Phone: 330-666-3711
www.wrhs.org/halefarm

The Homeplace
Land Between the Lakes
100 Van Morgan Drive
Golden Pond, KY 42211
Phone: 270-924-2000
www2.lbl.org/lbl/HPGate.html

Lincoln Log Cabin
State Historic Site
400 S. Lincoln Highway Road
P.O. Box 100
Lerna, IL 62440
Phone: 217-345-1845
www.lincolnlogcabin.org

Lincoln's New Salem
State Historic Site
Petersburg, IL 62675
Phone: 217-632-4000
www.lincolnsnewsalem.com

Living History Farms
2600 111th Street
Urbandale, IA, 50322
Phone: 515-278-2400
www.lhf.org

Naper Settlement
523 South Webster Street
Naperville, IL 60540
Phone: 630-420-6010
www.napersettlement.org

Old World Wisconsin
S103 W37890 Highway 67
Eagle, WI 53119
Phone: 262-594-6300
www.wisconsinhistory.org

Sauder Village
22611 State Route 2
P.O. Box 235
Archbold, OH 43502
Phone: 1-800-590-9755
or 419-446-2541
www.saudervillage.org

Index

About the Author

The author and illustrator of over eighty books for children and adults, **Raymond Bial** is best known for his versatility in portraiture, landscape, and still-life photography. His photo-essays for children include *Corn Belt Harvest, County Fair, Amish Home, Frontier Home, Shaker Home, The Underground Railroad, Portrait of a Farm Family, With Needle and Thread: A Book About Quilts, Mist Over the Mountains: Appalachia and Its People, Cajun Home, One-Room School, Where Lincoln Walked, Ghost Towns of the American West, A Handful of Dirt, Tenement: Immigrant Life on the Lower East Side*, and many others. His series of books include Building America and Lifeways, an acclaimed series about Native-American people. He has published three works of fiction for children: *The Fresh Grave and Other Ghostly Stories, The Ghost of Honeymoon Creek*, and *Shadow Island*. He lives in Urbana, Illinois, with his wife and children.